J.R. SWANTEK

Raising Pomskies

Breed Specific Tips From Puppy To Pomsky

First published by Swan Publishing LLC 2024

Copyright © 2024 by J.R. Swantek

All rights reserved. No part of this publication may be reproduced, stored or transmitted in any form or by any means, electronic, mechanical, photocopying, recording, scanning, or otherwise without written permission from the publisher. It is illegal to copy this book, post it to a website, or distribute it by any other means without permission.

J.R. Swantek asserts the moral right to be identified as the author of this work.

J.R. Swantek has no responsibility for the persistence or accuracy of URLs for external or third-party Internet Websites referred to in this publication and does not guarantee that any content on such Websites is, or will remain, accurate or appropriate.

Designations used by companies to distinguish their products are often claimed as trademarks. All brand names and product names used in this book and on its cover are trade names, service marks, trademarks and registered trademarks of their respective owners. The publishers and the book are not associated with any product or vendor mentioned in this book. None of the companies referenced within the book have endorsed the book.

This publication is designed to provide accurate and authoritative information in regard to the subject matter covered. It is sold with the understanding that neither the author nor the publisher is engaged in rendering legal, investment, accounting or other professional services. While the publisher and author have used their best efforts in preparing this book, they make no representations or warranties with respect to the accuracy or completeness of the contents of this book and specifically disclaim any implied warranties of merchantability or fitness for a particular purpose. No warranty may be created or extended by sales representatives or written sales materials. The advice and strategies contained herein may not be suitable for your situation. You should consult with a professional when appropriate. Neither the publisher nor the author shall be liable for any loss of profit or any other commercial damages, including but not limited to special, incidental, consequential, personal, or other damages.

First edition

ISBN: 978-1-965962-00-8

Cover art by J.R. Swantek

This book was professionally typeset on Reedsy.
Find out more at reedsy.com

This book is dedicated to Pac-Man, the Pomsky that started it all!

Contents

Introduction	1
Is This Book for You?	1
What is a Pomsky?	1
Who is Pac-Man?	3
1 Pre-Puppy Must Dos	5
Shopping List	5
Pet Proofing	9
Logistics	11
2 Adoption Week aka Hell Week	12
First Impressions Last	12
Scheduling Chaos	13
Teeth, Teeth, and More Teeth	14
3 Puppy Phase	15
Crate Training	15
Potty Training	16
Let's Do Tricks	17
4 Next Level Training	20
Socializing	20
Puppy School	21
Exercise	21
5 Pomsky Health	23
Breed Specific Diet Tips	24
Floof, Floof, and More Floof	25
No Fixed Schedule for Fixing	26

6 Teenage Angst	28
Coping with New Fears	28
Tricks for Stubborn Days	29
Grow the Pack	31
7 Full Grown Little Wolf	32
Are You Smarter Than a Dog?	32
Alpha Instincts	33
Young at Heart	34
8 Reflection	35
9 Reference List	37
About the Author	40

Introduction

Is This Book for You?

If you picked up this book, chances are you already adopted a Pomsky. Or perhaps you are considering getting a Pomsky. Or maybe, like me, it is your lifelong dream to have a Pomsky in your life. Either way this book is for you.

If you are considering getting a dog but don't know what breed you will get or even think a Pomsky isn't for you, then this book might still be for you. I can't promise you'll get the same value as an aspiring Pomsky owner, but a lot of the information could be relevant to other breeds of dogs.

And if you just bought this book because my mom wouldn't stop pestering you and bragging about how I finally published a book...well, then this book probably isn't for you. But I do greatly appreciate your support!

What is a Pomsky?

A Pomsky is a designer hybrid dog. It is the result of breeding a Husky and a Pomeranian. It is essentially a miniature Husky. Some Pomskies may take on more of the Pomeranian look but for the most part they look like small wolves. Their coat, eye color, and features all depend on the mixture of genetics so all 6 of our Pomskies have different coat color and thickness, different eye colors, and different markings. They certainly don't look like any kind of wolf pack you would find in the wild.

Puppies being advertised as Pomskies have an adult size range of 8 lbs to 60 lbs with the average weight being 25 lbs. Anything below 15 lbs and under 10 inches tall at the shoulder is considered a toy size (American Pomsky Kennel Club, 2023). As a breeder, we have only ever had two toy size Pomskies. Our smallest was a beautiful all white, blue eyed Pomsky weighing only 8 lbs as a full-grown adult. Our first generation Pomskies are ~20 lbs while all their second-generation children (2 Pomskies bred together naturally) weigh between 8 lbs and 16 lbs.

A first generation Pomsky is conceived by artificially inseminating a female Husky with Pomeranian semen (American Pomsky Kennel Club, 2023). This is best accomplished with a pure-bred Husky and a pure-bred Pomeranian. Ideally, both the bitch and the stud would possess high quality genes for their respective breed. And preferably, they would have no evidence of genetic health issues.

Pomskies are not recognized as an official breed by the American Kennel Club (AKC) due to the inconsistencies of their genetic makeup and lack of generational depth needed to establish firm breed traits (American Pomsky Kennel Club, 2019). The American Pomsky Kennel Club (APKC) is its own organization that is working with the AKC to establish the breed. The APKC will accept Pomskies that also contain American Eskimo genes and small traces of other genes (American Pomsky Kennel Club, 2023).

INTRODUCTION

Who is Pac-Man?

Pac-Man is the leader of the 8-Bit Pomsky Pack. That is what we call our little wolf pack of misfits. That's not exactly true because the real alpha of the pack is Atari (Pac-Man's wife), but she does let him pretend to be the leader.

Let's try this again... Pac-Man was the first Pomsky to join our little family. He is the gorgeous first-generation Pomsky featured on the cover of this book. He used to fit in my wife's sweater but now he is 20 lbs of graceful floof.

We got Pac-Man while we were living in Columbus, OH in a shoe box apartment right before the start of the COVID era. Since we lived in a 3rd floor walk up and were unable to venture away from the apartment complex except to the nearby city park, he is the most well-trained dog I have ever owned.

He became such an integral part of our family that we decided to get another Pomsky. And the rest is history. Since Pac-Man was born of a pure-bred Husky and pure-bred Pomeranian, he has perfect genes for breeding second-generation Pomskies. His DNA is a perfect 50/50 mix of the 2 breeds (Embark, 2021) which has led us to produce puppies well below the average weight of Pomskies advertised in the market and some with rare coat colorings.

He had two litters with his wife, Atari, each with four puppies. And another litter with his mistress, a female Pomsky from another breeder, with eight puppies. We kept two puppies from the first litter, one from the second litter, and one from his mistress. So now we have six Pomskies!

Taking care of six full-grown Pomskies is enough work. So, we have retired from full-scale breeding. We still have Pac-Man and Kirby (his rare-coated bastard child) available for stud services. But no more teeny tiny wolf packs wandering around our house terrorizing Atari and my wife.

We have decided to share what we've learned about the breed from Pac-Man and the rest of the 8-Bit Pomsky Pack by way of this book. We hope you will find the book entertaining and educational.

1

Pre-Puppy Must Dos

Before your Pomsky can join your family, there are quite a few things you should consider doing. You don't have to do these things as sometimes a puppy walks into your life unexpectedly and you can't say no. That's how we got Pac-Man.

A couple days before Christmas, I took my sister to a pet store to show her a beautiful chocolate colored Pomsky I had seen the week before. She was no longer there, but we met Pac-Man, and we fell in love. We ended up taking him home that day. So, we did not do any of the pre-puppy must dos and we learned some lessons the hard way.

With each new Pomsky we got better about doing the prep work. Here is a chance to learn from our mistakes.

Shopping List

Here is a table you can use for buying supplies for your new Pomsky puppy. The must haves are things I recommend purchasing before you bring your puppy home. The should haves are things that you don't need on day one but will need at some point so go ahead and buy them if you can.

Must Haves

Dog Crate
Crate training is an essential part of the Pomsky raising process. They descend from den animals (Smyth, 2022) and need a safe space to call their own.

Small Blanket
This is for inside the crate. Pomskies tend to destroy pillows. A blanket provides them comfort but allows them the flexibility to move it around and claw at it. They can adjust it to find their perfect laying spot.

Large Blanket
Pomskies are den animals. They like to have a dark place to retreat to, like a cave. We always keep a blanket on their crates and have the doors open so they can retreat to their safe space whenever they like.

Bell for Door
Pomskies are incredibly smart but also incredibly stubborn. Using potty training bells allows them to tell you when they need to go outside to go potty.

Puppy Food
I suggest having multiple puppy foods on hand. Pomskies are picky eaters, and it might take you a couple tries to find the right fit. At some point, your puppy will get bored with its food, and you can switch things up. We have had success using grain free food to prevent itchy skin.

PRE-PUPPY MUST DOS

Slow Feeder

Pomskies love food. Until they reach an age where they can self-regulate and graze, it is best to use a slow feeder. This will also help stimulate their mind during feeding times. We recommend breaking the daily food amount into two meals per day for a puppy.

Water Bowl

If possible, a water fountain style bowl is the best. But watch out! Pomskies love to chew wires and if they eat the power cord that fountain bowl becomes just a bowl.

Teething Toy

A Pomsky puppy will chew on anything. Pac-Man once tried to eat the corner of the wall. If you want to keep your security deposit, I suggest having plenty of teething tows on hand.

Dog Leash

Your puppy is going to need to go potty and is going to need to go on walks. Whether you have a fenced yard or not, it is best to start out on a leash. This will allow you to keep your puppy near you and out of harm's way.

Heartbeat Pillow

Unless your new puppy is older than the normal adoption age, your Pomsky is going to be used to sleeping with other dogs. Whether it's the mother or its siblings, it is used to the heat and heartbeat of another body. If you want to get some sleep, help your puppy sleep by giving them the comfort of a heartbeat pillow with heated insert.

Poop Bags

Don't be that person. Pick up after your Pomsky.

Should Haves

Training Treats

Pomskies are incredibly smart, and they can learn a lot if you start them at an early age. We like to use Little Jacs for training, but our dogs also love organic teddy graham style dog treats and cheerios.

Clicker

We encourage positive reinforcement training techniques. A clicker allows you to signify a good job without a treat and is an important tool for training a Pomsky if you don't have an unlimited treat budget.

Ball

Pomskies have a lot of energy. And not just as a puppy. They will always need a lot of exercise. A ball is a great way to play and get exercise. They are good at fetch and as they get older can learn to even catch the ball. That being said, if you get tennis balls, don't leave them unattended. Your puppy will eat the hide of the ball and then shred the internal rubber part.

Puzzle Toy

Pomskies are incredibly smart. It is your job to keep their mind stimulated. If not, they will find their own way - usually by destroying something. When Pac-Man was a puppy, we used to put pig ears in a rubber buckyball. He eventually outsmarted that and had to graduate to more challenging toys.

Dog Food Bin

It is best to store dog food in a sealed container with a scoop rather than in the bags. Most bags aren't resealable, and they are an odd shape to store. Without a bin, you have to store the dog food out of reach because a Pomsky will figure out how to get into the bag and will overeat. Nobody enjoys a trip to the emergency vet to make sure the puppy didn't flip its stomach and to get fluids.

Dog Bed
Pomskies love to have a comfortable place to lie down, and a dog bed can be a good training tool as well. Just be cautious of what bed you get as the puppy will claw at it to get comfortable. Once the stuffing is visible, all bets are off! The puppy will pull every last piece of stuffing out of a dog bed, pillow, or even a stuffed toy.

Harness
A leash is great but attaching it to a collar is less than ideal. It is not good for your puppy's neck and doesn't give you the best control during walks. Consider a harness where the leash clips to the puppy's back and provides both a holder for the poop bags and reflectors to keep your Pomsky visible in the dark.

Pet Proofing

A Pomsky is part Husky. That is a dog breed so smart they can be trained to work as a team and pull a full-grown human and gear on a sled. Pomskies are miniature Huskies. Just as smart and just as much energy in a dog only a third of the size. If you don't keep them on the go and mentally stimulated, they get bored. A bored Pomsky puppy will cause mayhem in your home.

Before you bring your puppy home, it is important to pet proof your house. Kind of like baby proofing but instead of trying to protect the baby you are trying to protect the house. Here are the main 3 things to consider for proofing your home:

1) Anything on the floor is fair game

If the puppy can reach it, it will find it. It will likely chew on it. And it will likely destroy it. If there is something you don't want your Pomsky to eat, don't leave it where they can reach it. This applies to things you use every day and might not think about such as TV remotes. We still have to point our remote at a weird angle to get the signal to pass correctly. As your Pomsky gets older it will develop an incredible jumping ability. But while it is still a puppy, counters and tables are your best friend.

2) Wires are Pomsky puppy magnets

Something about a wire just speaks to a Pomsky's soul. It doesn't matter if it is a loose wire or if it is plugged into the wall. If your Pomsky puppy can reach it, it will chew on it. This is probably one of the most dangerous things about a Pomsky puppy. Unidentified chewed wires plugged into a power source are a fire hazard. If your puppy goes beyond chewing and eats parts of wires, it can be very bad for its health. So, make sure you put away your phone chargers, headphones, and laptop wires. And also, be sure to tuck any permanent wires such as TV wires behind a piece of furniture that your puppy doesn't fit behind or under.

3) Contain the chaos

Like a baby, it is best not to leave a Pomsky puppy unattended. Your puppy will behave better when you are around and giving them attention. Crate training is incredibly important for this reason. If you can't pay attention to the puppy for the next hour or two, put them in their crate for nap. This will also help with building bladder control and independence.

Our Pomskies love their crates and use them all the time as a safe space to nap. If you aren't comfortable with using the crate outside of bedtime, then I suggest setting up some sort of playpen area where there is nothing for the puppy to get into. Just be prepared to clean up after the not yet potty-trained puppy makes a mess on the playpen floor. And also know, it won't take long before the puppy figures out how to get out of the playpen and run a muck in the rest of the house.

Logistics

In addition to shopping and pet proofing, there are some logistics you should consider before bringing home a Pomsky puppy. For starters, you should try to plan your first week being a time when you don't have to go to work. A puppy's first week is what we call Hell Week. We will discuss it further in Chapter 2. But trust me, you don't want to have to go into the office during Hell Week. So, schedule it during a holiday or vacation. If you can't do a whole week, then at least start on a weekend. Preferably a long weekend.

Next, you want to make sure your home is set up to help you in the transition process. The dog crate needs to be set up with the blankets, the bells should be on the door, and the leash and comfortable shoes should be readily accessible. You don't want to be fumbling around in the dark, tripping over new puppy toys, and searching for a leash when your Pomsky wakes you in the middle of the night needing to go potty.

When you bring a puppy to your home, it's like taking a child to a hotel for the first time. They are going to act up, get into mischief, jump on the bed, and then have trouble sleeping. Your home is a foreign land to the puppy, and you have just taken them away from everything they have ever known. The puppy is going to have a hard time sleeping and will wake you up or go potty in the crate. It is important to set up an environment that makes your puppy feel at home in your home.

2

Adoption Week aka Hell Week

The week you adopt your Pomsky and bring them into your home is going to be chaos. I know because I have been through it. We call it Hell Week and we have lived through it multiple times. There is no way around it. You just have to get through it. Here are some tips that will help you navigate this critical time in your Pomsky's development.

First Impressions Last

Hell Week is a week of firsts. Everything that happens with your Pomsky that week is going to be a first. First feeding time, first potty time, first bedtime...you get the picture. It is easy to get caught up in the emotion of having a new puppy and the chaos of all the changes. But you must pay close attention to all the firsts. Try to avoid letting them slip by you.

Pomskies are smart. Your puppy is going to notice everything that happens during their first week in your house. They are going to test you and push your boundaries. You must establish the rules and stick to them. If you want your puppy to do tricks at feeding time or use a command word for food, you should do it from the first feeding time. If you want your puppy to ring the bells before potty time, you should help them ring the bells before the first potty time. Be selective about what you do and do not reward with treats because they are watching.

Scheduling Chaos

The first week is going to be chaos so scheduling is everything. You start by scheduling when the first week is going to be. During a holiday or vacation is preferable so you can give your undivided attention to your Pomsky. That is not always possible. So, make sure you start on a weekend and at the very least, do not schedule it during your busiest time of year.

During Hell Week, you want to schedule everything. This is going to help your Pomsky adapt to its new home and help keep you sane. Scheduling feeding times will help regulate when your puppy needs to go potty. Scheduling walking times will encourage your puppy to build bladder control and wait for walking time to pee. Scheduling nap time will give you time to get things done without having to supervise the puppy. Nap time will also help your Pomsky get used to their crate and consider it a safe space.

Like humans, dogs have an internal biological clock. The more you condition that clock during the first week, the more your puppy's schedule will be adapted to your own. As such, it is important that you stick to your schedule unless you are making an active change. Keeping strict to your schedule will establish boundaries for your puppy. An understanding of your boundaries and that they do not waiver is a fundamental tool in the remainder of your puppy's training.

Teeth, Teeth, and More Teeth

Your Pomsky is descended from predators and, like its Husky parent, has kept some behavioral traits from its ancestors (Primitivedogs Team, 2015). Pomskies have a natural drive to use their teeth. They are going to want to chew on everything. It is your job to give them healthy and safe things to chew on, so they don't find their own alternatives. When they inevitably do find their own alternatives, it is your job to teach them that is a "no-no".

Puppy teething toys are of course a no brainer. But there are plenty of other options and tools to consider. Our Pomskies are fond of ice. We find it is best to make our own frozen treats, so they aren't just eating water. With the right tools, ice and frozen treats can be used for licking which will not stop teething but will help soothe the gums.

If you would like to give your dog a bone to chew on, make sure you do your research. Dog teeth can handle different levels of hardness at different ages. Most bones we've seen are too hard for puppy teeth. We recommend a cow knuckle. The inside of the bone is soft enough for puppies to chew at and it will keep them entertained and stimulate their mind. As the puppy gets older, it will be able to chew on the harder parts of the cow knuckle.

Another tip for keeping your Pomsky's teething under control is to brush their teeth. It is important to get your puppy comfortable with you touching their face at an early age as it might be necessary for health and safety reasons at some point in their life. This means touching their ears, eyes, nose, and inside their mouth. The best way to get them used to you touching inside their mouth is to use your finger to brush their teeth. This can have the added benefit of soothing their gums, so they are less inclined to bite things.

3

Puppy Phase

A Pomsky has a long puppy phase. Your puppy will be a puppy for a whole year. Around the six-month mark, your Pomsky will go through its first full scale coat shed. It is easy to mistake this as adulthood because your Pomsky will look very different. But trust me, your Pomsky will still be a puppy. It will take the rest of the puppy year to grow back full Pomsky hair and return to a similar look as the day you brought your puppy home.

A Pomsky is most teachable when it is a puppy. There are some things you are definitely going to want to focus your training on during the first year. I have broken them down for you here.

Crate Training

Crate training is one of the most important things for a Pomsky puppy. Your Pomsky needs to be comfortable spending time in a crate. Crate training will directly impact your ability potty train your puppy, your ability to get things done around the house, your ability to leave the house without your puppy, and your ability to get some sleep.

Some people are against crates and think it is cruel to dogs. For a

Pomsky, a crate is essential. It is where they nap. It is where they sleep. It is their safe space. Being a descendant of den animals, your Pomsky will treat their create like a den. But you do need to make sure you set up the crate correctly.

Make sure you buy a large enough crate. The crate should be large enough that your puppy would feel comfortable laying within one half. This way during the puppy year you can put a small blanket on one half and puppy pad on the other half in case of accidents. It also ensures that your puppy will have one den as it grows up and not have to get reacquainted with a new safe space.

If you keep your Pomsky's crate in the same place, keep it clean, keep the blanket clean, and keep it covered with a larger thin blanket, then your puppy will love its den. All six of our Pomskies still use their crates whenever they want to feel safe. You must keep the door open so they can choose to go in there. Our Pomskies sleep in their crates every night. If you say "night night" in our house, it is like a tornado of floof as all of them go flying by into their crates for a good night's rest.

It is important to properly use the crate for training. The crate is your dog's safe space. It should not be used as a punishment, and you should never try to remove your puppy from the crate if they don't want to come out. You have to build up your puppy's comfort with the crate using treats and naps so they know they can go in there not just for bedtime. Try putting your puppy in the crate with the door open and see how long they stay in there.

Potty Training

Pomskies are stubborn dogs! So, potty training can be a challenge. However, their stubbornness is a side effect of their intelligence. This is why bells will be your most important training tool for potty training. A set of jingle bells that hang from your door handle allow your Pomsky to tell you when they need to go outside to potty. The bells are just one part of the equation though.

Keep in mind it will take time for your Pomsky to learn bladder control. Frequent potty breaks will be necessary. It is best to start with breaks every hour or so and build up the time between potty breaks incrementally. You can use the crate to help you extend the time between potty breaks at least once per day for nap time.

It is important to remember that your puppy cannot let themselves outside. So, you will need to pay attention and let them out regularly. Most accidents happen from a puppy who can no longer hold it in. Once you train your puppy with the bells, they will know that outside is where they are supposed to go potty. This will be rather evident with your Pomsky because they will be ashamed and hide in their crate when they have an accident. So, try not to leave them unattended and have their leash and harness ready to go quickly.

Patience is the key to potty training. You will need to practice patience when they have an accident. And you will need to practice patience when you walk your puppy. They will not poop on command no matter how cold it is outside. It takes time to learn your Pomsky's walking preferences.

Let's Do Tricks

The puppy phase is the best time to teach a Pomsky all the basic tricks. Their intelligence makes them capable of a lot of tricks. They can do quite complex tricks, but they need a solid training foundation and basic tricks to build upon. For example, Pac-Man can stop, sit down, and look both ways before crossing the street. But first he had to learn to follow verbal commands, walk on a leash, and the basic trick of sit.

It doesn't happen overnight. But it can happen quite quickly with enough repetition. Feeding time and walking time are great opportunities to get trick repetition without needing training treats. If you feed your puppy twice per day, you can have them do up to four tricks plus a command word before they eat. For most of our Pomskies it was sit, high five, and lay down. Their command word was pellets in honor of Pac-Man. The command word teaches them both verbal commands as well as how to wait for a command.

Every time you walk your Pomsky is another opportunity for trick repetition. You can have a puppy do up to two tricks every walk before reentering your home. For ours it was sit and high five. This repetition builds the skill very quickly. At the end of a walk, your puppy will want nothing more than to get inside and off the leash.

It won't be long before your Pomsky is proactively doing the tricks when approaching the door. Then you can switch up the tricks if you want. Don't let your puppy outsmart you! When you reenter your home, you should always have your puppy sit before removing the leash. This is an important trick repetition because it also ensures you have time to close the door before removing the leash. Nobody wants to chase an unleashed puppy around outside.

Repetition will help the skills stick but you must teach them right the first time. It is important to use positive reinforcement to train tricks outside of the repetition opportunities. Training sessions should be impromptu and always use both treats and the clicker to reinforce successful behavior.

Consistency is the key to teaching the basic tricks of sit, high five, and lay down. You need to use the same commands every time for each trick. It is best to use both a verbal command and a hand signal. This will allow you to continue to give commands to your puppy in situations where either a verbal command is inappropriate, or hand signals are unable to be seen. Make sure to always reward a trick with either a click from the clicker or a treat. Your Pomsky is going to be doing lots of tricks. Make sure you pick a treat that is small and comes in large quantities.

4

Next Level Training

Training your Pomsky goes beyond just potty time and basic tricks. The goal of training your puppy is to provide the skills needed to behave in different situations. Your puppy needs to understand how to interact with different people and other animals. Otherwise, your Pomsky's life will be limited to your home and your typical walking path. This would be such a sad fate for such an intelligent and high-spirited companion.

Socializing

It is important to socialize your Pomsky with other dogs so they can learn appropriate behavior in a controlled setting. It is best to start with dogs you know either from friends and family or from your neighborhood. It will take time for your puppy to learn social skills and they may be either shy, scared, overly excited, or aggressive at first. This is why it is important to control the start of the interaction, so another dog does not surprise your puppy.

You do not start with a dog park. I do not recommend taking your puppy to a dog park until they are at least six months old and preferably not until they have been fixed. This is to protect your puppy before it has all the necessary shots. It will also help you learn your Pomsky's social appetite before exposing them to a less controllable environment. Signing your Pomsky up for puppy school is a really great way to socialize your puppy with other dogs and people in a controlled environment.

Puppy School

Most major pet stores offer puppy classes. If you can't find one near you, consider finding a group class with a private dog trainer. Puppy school doesn't offer anything revolutionary. Most things about training dogs you can now find online or in books. But I highly encourage signing up for training school.

Training your puppy is like any goal you set. It will take however long you give yourself to do it. Signing up for puppy school puts your training on a timeline and gives it structure. It also has the added bonus of being one of the most controllable environments to socialize your Pomsky with multiple other dogs. Since it takes place at a pet store, you can even expose your dog to other pets they may encounter at some point in their life.

Exercise

A Pomsky is a high energy dog breed. It may not always seem like it because they love naps, but they also love play time. Exercise is a great way to expand your puppy's training. You can have your Pomsky join your exercise such as running or walking. This would expose them to new locations beyond their shorter potty time walking path.

You can also plan some exercise activities for your Pomsky. Games like fetch and agility training help stimulate your puppy's mind while also burning some energy. Helping your puppy burn energy in a safe and stimulating way will help other parts of your training go more smoothly.

5

Pomsky Health

It is important to speak with your vet about proper preventive maintenance and care for your puppy. That being said, there are also some health considerations you should understand about your Pomsky. Since a Pomsky is a hybrid of a Pomeranian and a Husky, it is susceptible to genetic health concerns for both breeds.

Not all Pomskies will inherit genetic health concerns. It is possible your puppy will not be at risk for any of them. But it is important to understand the possibilities in order to make easy adjustments that will better your Pomsky's life. If you are overly concerned, I would encourage you to get a DNA test done for your Pomsky. We utilize Embark for testing ours.

Here are the potential health concerns for each breed. Remember your Pomsky carries genes from both breeds.

Husky (Paul, 2023):
Cataracts, Progressive Retinal Atrophy (PRA), Corneal Dystrophy, Hypothyroidism, and Hip Dysplasia

Pomeranian (Madden, 2022):

Hypoglycemia, Dry Eye, Tear Duct Issues, Cataracts, Distichiasis, Collapsing Trachea, Bronchodilators, Dental Disease, Hip Dysplasia, Legg-Calve-Perthes Disease, and Patellar Luxation

Breed Specific Diet Tips

Pomskies are picky eaters. You are going to want to make sure you have a couple different dog foods and treats on hand in the early stages until you learn what your puppy likes. For the long term, try to find a consistent brand that you trust that offers options. Being able to switch between different ingredients and different pellet shapes and sizes every couple of weeks will make feeding time go more smoothly.

Pomskies inherit some allergen concerns to grains, certain proteins, and food additives from the Pomeranian side (Sarah, 2024). It can cause them to itch and scratch more often. Because of this, we recommend providing your dog with grain free food and using organic grain products in the treats. Not really a diet tip, but nothing is more adorable than a Pomsky eating a pup-cup.

For other genetic health concerns such as hip issues in Huskies, there are dietary supplements available at the pet store. Some are pills which your Pomsky may or may not do well with taking, but others are powder that your sprinkle over their food. Not all of our 6 Pomskies like the pills, but they all enjoy the powder on their food. It is best to consult with a vet before providing your Pomsky with any health supplements.

Floof, Floof, and More Floof

If you don't like dog hair, then a Pomsky might not be the right breed for you. If you are allergic to dog hair, I would recommend enjoying this particular breed from afar. As a Pomsky parent, you get to enjoy dog hair on your floor, on your furniture, in your air filter, on your clothes, in your clothes, on your face, and even in your mouth.

Floof, floof everywhere! It will become such a normal part of your life that you won't even notice it anymore. Until one day, your friend will visit and have a crazy asthma attack by just sitting on your couch. Or you will wear a black article of clothing outside of your home and not remember why you have removed that color from your wardrobe until it is too late. There's never a lint roller around when you need one...unless you are a Pomsky owner. We keep a lint roller in most rooms of our house and in every car.

Pomsky hair care is going to be an important part of your pet care routine. The Pomsky coat will shed similarly to the Husky breed. You can plan on two sheds per year (Embark, 2024). Most likely they will be seasonal such as start of summer and winter. Because of this, you can usually plan ahead for the shedding seasons. Although sometimes they will get tripped up if you have fake spring followed by a cold snap. You can accidentally trigger an extra shed if you and your Pomsky vacation somewhere tropical during the winter. So, plan accordingly. You do not want to do that to yourself on vacation without the proper tools.

There are a lot of tools available for managing the shedding season. For starters, you will definitely want to acquire some sort of lint roller or pet hair removal device. You will use these often on clothes and furniture. You should also consider vacuuming, sweeping, and changing your air filter more often than in a typical household. Some air filters and vacuums do better with pet hair so make sure you do your research.

The number one tool in the fight against the floof is a de-shedding brush. Your best defensive against floof is a strong offense. We recommend brushing your Pomsky with this type of brush daily. This does two things: (1) keeps the daily shedding contained and easy to dispose and (2) conditions your Pomsky to expect or even enjoy being brushed so they do not resist during shedding season.

If you really want to combat the spreading of the floof, my parents have had success with bathing their Pomsky at least once per week. The bath alone will remove a lot of loose hair and stop it from getting all over the place. Using de-shedding shampoo will increase the impact of the baths. Since we have 6 Pomskies we cannot bathe them all weekly. We have succumbed to the floof. Save yourself and heed our guidance.

There are two more tools to consider in the war on floof. Both require you to get your Pomsky used to their respective noises at an early age, so they do not fear them. During the shedding season, you can blow out your dog's hair outside using a leaf blower. This is best done when you are certain they are in full shed mode and best done in conjunction with a bath. The other tool is a vacuum brush. This tool will allow you to suck up the dog hair as you brush your Pomsky. If your dog is comfortable with the noise, this tool can be very effective in controlling the spread of the floof.

No Fixed Schedule for Fixing

As your Pomsky gets older, you are going to want to get them fixed. This is necessary for using some dog related services such as boarding, doggy daycare, and even some dog parks. I would encourage you to wait if you can.

Some pet stores and breeders set an expectation of getting your puppy fixed at six months. Some people recommend waiting until they lose their first baby canine tooth. This typically happens for Pomskies around

9 months in my experience. I recommend waiting until you are confident your Pomsky has grown into their full adult coat. This is around one to one and a half years.

You might think your Pomsky is full grown at a year, but not quite. They will have gained most of their weight and size by one year. But the last ten percent of their weight will come over the course of the second year as they finish filling out their coat and build. If you can wait until your Pomsky is full grown, they will appear with a more natural full coat and build if not fixed too early.

6

Teenage Angst

Teenage angst is not exclusive to humans. Unfortunately, this does not mean your Pomsky is going to start listening to your favorite alternative rock bands. Nor will they start sporting weird styles or fashion trends that they might end up regretting later. That right of passage is exclusive to dog's best friend. Your Pomsky may however develop some typical signs of teenage angst such as restlessness, moodiness, lack of energy, changes of appetite, and inexplicable fears (Quinn, 2023).

Coping with New Fears

It will be an important focus of yours during the teen years to help your Pomsky cope with and eventually overcome their new fears. Just like those awkward teen years we all try to forget; your puppy is going to go through transformations that make them uncomfortable in their own body. The challenge for you will be that they will have reached a new level of cuteness.

You will want to play with them, snuggle them, and take them places to show them off. But they may not want to do those things. You will need to practice patience and stay observant to help them through this phase. It will be important to control scenarios in which your Pomsky is exposed to their newfound fears. They need to know that you are there to protect them and keep them safe.

For example, one of our Pomskies became afraid of meeting new people and other dogs. He would shyly hide behind my wife and sometimes would even growl. This was not handled by forcing him to meet new people and dogs. It was handled delicately. We allowed him to come to meet new people at his own pace. We controlled scenarios where new dogs would meet him and made sure it wasn't from a position where he felt exposed.

If you are not observant, you might not notice some of the new fears. Through your natural actions, you may inadvertently cause your Pomsky some trauma. Imagine you were afraid of spiders and your parents put a spider on your head. You might be scarred for life. It might seem silly, but that might be exactly how your teenage Pomsky feels when you put their collar on. Remember to pay attention, handle with care, and practice patience and I am sure your Pomsky will overcome their new fears in no time.

Tricks for Stubborn Days

It may seem counter intuitive, but the stubborn days of the teen years are a great time to teach your Pomsky new tricks. Training by nature requires a lot of one-on-one attention with your dog which is exactly what they need. You want to start by recapping old tricks which they should know well by now. You may have stopped rewarding tricks such as the basics as often as you used to with your puppy.

Pomskies are incredibly smart. While they will do the basic tricks consistently without an edible reward, they are bound to catch on eventually and start holding out for a treat. The treat to trick ratio typically reaches this critical point right around the teen years. This is an opportunity for you to renew trust and build up your relationship with positive reinforcement at a time when their personality may be shifting. So do not be stingy with the treats.

It can be difficult to teach your Pomsky overly complex tricks during stubborn days. I would not use a dog show for my inspiration. Instead, root the new tricks in the basics. Expand on the basics to slightly more impressive tricks. This will help you get some wins quickly. It will also help you set an expectation of continued learning that is necessary to achieve those seemingly impossible complex tricks in later years.

Here are some examples of extending what your Pomsky should already know into a more complex trick:

- Bow – an extension of lay down
- I Love You – an extension of speak
- Dance – an extension of stand
- Patty Cake – an extension of high five
- Stay – an extension of wait
- Crate – an extension of bedtime
- Catch – an extension of fetch

You can also string some of the basics together with slight adjustments to make more complex tricks. A great example of this was the Stop and Look trick I alluded to earlier. By combing verbal commands and visual cues with the basic tricks of sit and wait, I was able to teach Pac-Man and Atari how to stop and look both ways when we came to a road. Other strings of basic tricks might include things like play dead which combines stand, lay down, and roll over or beg which combines sit, paw, and speak.

Grow the Pack

Pomskies descend from Huskies which were natural pack animals before being domesticated (Primitivedogs Team, 2015). If you watch them in a group, they start to develop a pack mentality. I am not going to recommend everyone adopt six Pomskies. This life is certainly not for everyone even though a Pomsky dog pile is the most adorable and awesome thing I've ever experienced. I will however recommend that you get your Pomsky a companion if they do not already have one by the time they reach their teen years.

The other members of the pack do not have to be a Pomsky. They do not even have to be a little dog. We have seen our Pomskies get along well with some of the largest dog breeds. Having a second dog is an important step in the socialization and development of your Pomsky.

Pomskies are high energy pack animals. If you choose not to expand the pack, I hope you can adopt a lifestyle that meets their physical needs. They need lots of play time, exercise, and socialization. It will take a lot of time on your part to compensate for a lack of pack. And you still might need to provide a pseudo pack through doggy play dates and such.

We went to the opposite extreme with our Pomskies. With a pack our size, our biggest challenge is keeping them from going into full pack mode. We must remind them that they are domestic animals, that they cannot just do whatever they want, and that we also live in the house. It has been fun to watch the pack dynamics unfold, but nothing has been more rewarding than the moments they clearly show that we are part of the pack.

7

Full Grown Little Wolf

Before you know it, your little puppy will have transformed into a full-grown miniature wolf called a Pomsky. This bundle of floof will have the boundless energy of a rabbit, the pack mentality of a wolf, and the grace of a deer. These traits, paired with a high level of intelligence, make Pomskies one of the most challenging dogs to own. Their stubbornness can play on your last nerve. So, make sure you get as much training as possible done early if you can.

Are You Smarter Than a Dog?

You may be smarter than a 5th grader, but you might not be smarter than a Pomsky. Your Pomsky is going to keep you on your toes every day. In a challenge of wits between the Pomsky and the 5th grader, I am betting on the Pomsky every time.

The Pomsky breed descends from wolves and inherits a high level of intelligence (Primitivedogs Team, 2015). Their pack mentality makes them well equipped to learn from their surroundings. They are observant and will adjust their actions based on their observations of you. If you aren't as observant, they will be able to manipulate you. Like how a child can have their parents wrapped around their finger.

It will be important to continue to exercise your Pomsky's mind throughout adulthood. Keeping them engaged with mental challenges will ensure they use their intelligence to earn treats rather than torment you or others. Their high level of intelligence means they will experience complex emotions including getting offended by your actions. If you offend a Pomsky, their stubbornness will reach new heights, and they will take actions specifically to spite you.

Alpha Instincts

Never forget the genetic tendencies of your Pomsky. They don't just want to be in a pack, they want to lead the pack. They will push to be the alpha unless they have someone to follow. They will consider you a part of the pack. If you have raised them right, they will consider you the alpha. But you will have to continue to earn the right to be their leader.

Even though you are the alpha, you will still see your Pomsky exhibit alpha tendencies when with other dogs and animals. They will always challenge for the top position unless experience teaches them otherwise. Being a part of a pack and being an alpha goes beyond just wanting to be the leader. It is about devotion to family and protecting loved ones.

As the alpha, your Pomsky will expect you to care for the pack and defend it. If you fail at this duty, then your Pomsky may challenge your position. In such situations, your Pomsky will exhibit high levels of stubbornness and spiteful behavior. It is important to remain observant of your dog's emotions throughout its adult life. This will be essential to keep your Pomsky's trust and maintain a healthy relationship.

Young at Heart

Owning a Pomsky is a long-term commitment to a high energy lifestyle. Pomskies are like Peter Pan, they never grow up. They never slow down. Just when you think things are calm and they are spending the day napping, they get the zoomies and are a puppy again.

Keeping your Pomsky active and playful is essential to their long-term physical and emotional health. It is like protecting an inner child. If you keep your Pomsky's spark alive, then they will keep their puppy energy throughout their life. This can be the most difficult part to keep up with as an owner.

Humans are notoriously bad at keeping up with an exercise routine. We often let changes and stressors disrupt routines leading to long gaps in physical activity. This is why so many people make the gym a new year's resolution every year. Find a way to stay active for your dog's sake, if you have a Pomsky.

When you find yourself lacking the energy and drive, you can supplement the relationship with outside help. Play dates and dog parks are a great way to keep your dog active without requiring extensive physicality on your part. Games like fetch and tug-of-war can be done while you are sitting. So, don't let your slump impact your Pomsky. Let their never-ending energy keep you inspired to get moving.

8

Reflection

Once you've raised your puppy into a full grown Pomsky, it is important to take time to reflect on your journey. You may have some hard-earned lessons, but you should also have some cherished memories. Your reflection will be critical to guiding your relationship with your Pomsky for the rest of their hopefully long and happy lives.

If you still have time on your Pomsky journey, or perhaps haven't started it yet, then make sure to take time to reflect as you go. Plan time for reflection. Enjoy where you are on the journey. Take note of things that have gone well and things you need to work on with your Pomsky. This will help you make minor adjustments as you go. You want to reach the big reflections period with as many cherished memories and as few hard-earned lessons as possible.

After you reflect, share what you have learned. Not everyone has to make every mistake for themselves. Maybe they can learn from your mistakes or benefit from information about actions that led to your cherished memories. I have raised a whole pack of full-grown Pomskies, and I have played a crucial role in the raising of many others.

I hope you have enjoyed reading the outcome of my desire to share the knowledge identified in my own reflection. If you found this book helpful, I would appreciate it if you gave a favorable review on Amazon for the book!

9

Reference List

AKC Staff. (2024, May 14). The 7 AKC Dog Breed Groups Explained. Retrieved August 2024, from American Kennel Club: https://www.akc.org/expert-advice/lifestyle/7-akc-dog-breed-groups-explained/

American Kennel Club. (2024). About Clubs. Retrieved August 2024, from American Kennel Club: https://www.akc.org/clubs-delegates/clubs/about-clubs/

American Kennel Club. (2024). Club Relations Department. Retrieved August 2024, from American Kennel Club: https://www.akc.org/clubs-delegates/clubs/about-club-relations/

American Kennel Club. (2024). Pomeranian. Retrieved August 2024, from American Kennel Club: https://www.akc.org/dog-breeds/pomeranian/

American Kennel Club. (2024). Siberian Husky. Retrieved August 2024, from American Kennel Club: https://www.akc.org/dog-breeds/siberian-husky/

American Pomsky Kennel Club. (2019). AKC Recognition. Retrieved August 2024, from American Pomsky Kennel Club: https://americanpomskykennelclub.org/akc-recognition-requirements

American Pomsky Kennel Club. (2019). POMSKY - Is It a Good Fit for You? Retrieved August 2024, from American Pomsky Kennel Club: https://americanpomskykennelclub.org/pomsky-faq

American Pomsky Kennel Club. (2023). APKC Breed Standard. Retrieved August 2024, from American Pomsky Kennel Club: https://americanpomskykennelclub.org/apkc-standards-2023

Chesson, D. (2023, November 29). How to Build an Amazing "About the Author" Page. Retrieved August 2024, from Kindlepreneur: https://kindlepreneur.com/build-about-the-author-page/

Chesson, D. (2024, January 8). Guide to Writing a Book Copyright Page [With 6 Templates]. Retrieved August 2024, from Kindlepreneur: https://kindlepreneur.com/book-copyright-page-examples-ebook/

Embark. (2021, February 28). Pac-Man Tinsel Swantek DNA Test Report. Retrieved August 2024, from Embark: https://my.embarkvet.com/members/reports/print-report-pdf/LR6DP-MVLJ8-GDLVQ-83G5Z

Embark. (2024). Dog Breeds: Pomsky. Retrieved August 2024, from Embark: https://embarkvet.com/resources/dog-breeds/pomsky/

Madden, A. (2022, June 22). Pomeranian. Retrieved August 2024, from Pet MD by Chewy: https://www.petmd.com/dog/breeds/pomeranian

Paul, T. (2023, June 1). Siberian Husky. (B. J. Morrison, Editor) Retrieved

REFERENCE LIST

August 2024, from Pet MD by Chewy: https://www.petmd.com/dog/breeds/siberian-husky

Primitivedogs Team. (2015, June 22). History Of Huskies And Their Origin. Retrieved August 2024, from Primitive Dogs: https://primitivedogs.com/origin-and-history-of-huskies/?cn-reloaded=1

Quinn, D. (2023, November 9). Teen Angst: 11+ Causes, Symptoms, & When You Should be Concerned. (S. Fletcher, Editor) Retrieved August 2024, from Sandstone Care: https://www.sandstonecare.com/blog/teen-angst/

Sarah. (2024, January 21). Understanding Pomeranian Allergies: A Comprehensive Guide. Retrieved August 2024, from Pomeranian Dogs: https://pomeraniandogs.org/pomeranian-allergies/

Smyth, M. (2022, May 12). Your Guide To Where Huskies Like To Sleep? (Some places might surprise you). Retrieved August 2024, from My Perfect Doggy: https://myperfectdoggy.com/your-guide-to-where-huskies-like-to-sleep/#Where_Do_Huskies_Sleep_In_The_Wild

About the Author

James is the founder of the 8-Bit Pomsky Pack. It was his lifelong dream to own a Pomsky. He has raised a whole pack of full-grown Pomskies and has played a crucial role in the raising of many others. He lives in Virginia with his wife and six Pomskies where he has created an outdoor adventure oasis to explore with his pack.

When he's not tending to the many needs of Pac-Man, Atari, Clyde, Ink-a-saurus, Kirby, and Pumpkin, he advocates for water technology and environmental education in the United States. He also has a passion for spoken word poetry and collecting fine art. Learn more about the Pack and their alpha by following them on social media using the links below.

You can connect with me on:
- https://www.linkedin.com/in/jamesswantek
- https://www.instagram.com/8bitpomskies

www.ingramcontent.com/pod-product-compliance
Lightning Source LLC
LaVergne TN
LVHW051205080426
835508LV00021B/2821